AF472044

One Liner's

1. My friend asked me if I was addicted to somersaults, and I said, "Nah, that's just how I roll!"
2. My friend asked me if I was addicted to brake fluid, and I said, "Nah, I can stop anytime!"
3. I stayed up all night studying for my urine test, and I passed!
4. My family has a predisposition for diarrhea... Runs in our jeans!
5. My wife and I were happy for twenty years. Then we met.
6. Just read that 4,153,237 people got married last year, not to cause any trouble but shouldn't that be an even number?
7. I'm great at multitasking. I can waste time, be unproductive, and procrastinate all at once!
8. I find it ironic that colors red, white, and blue stand for freedom until they are flashing behind you.
9. Feeling pretty proud of myself. The Sesame Street puzzle I bought said 3-5 years, but I finished it in 18 months.
10. My favorite mythical creature? The honest politician.
11. Take my advice- I'm not using it.
12. I changed my password to "incorrect". So whenever I forget what it is the computer will say, "Your password is incorrect".
13. Money talks... but all mine ever says is good-bye.
14. If you're not supposed to eat at night, why is there a light in the refrigerator?
15. Wi-Fi went down during family dinner tonight. One kid started talking and I didn't know who he was.
16. My resolution was to read more so I put the subtitles on my TV.
17. Thanks for explaining the word many to me. It means a lot.
18. Waking up this morning was an eye-opening experience.
19. If 4 out of 5 people suffer from diarrhea- does that mean one enjoys it?
20. Do you think that when they asked George Washington for ID, he just whipped out a quarter?
21. My dad never loved me as a child. I can't really blame him though. I wasn't born until he was an adult.
22. I tell ya, when I was a kid, all I knew was rejection. My yo-yo? It never came back.
23. I put a dollar in a change machine. Nothing changed.
24. If number two pencils are so popular, why are they still number two?
25. When I was a child, my father attacked me with cameras; I still have flashbacks!
26. I'm reading a book about antigravity- I just can't put it down!
27. You just can't trust atoms- they make up everything!
28. Before I criticize a man, I like to walk a mile in his shoes. That way, when I do criticize him, I'm a mile away and I have his shoes.
29. My wife had her driver's test the other day. She got 8 out of 10. The other 2 guys jumped clear.
30. A computer once beat me at chess, but it was no match for me at kick boxing.

31. If procrastination was an Olympic sport, I'd compete in it later.
32. Why is the day that you do laundry, cook, clean, iron, and so on, called a day off?
33. Escalators don't break down… they just turn into stairs.
34. Whoever said nothing is impossible is a liar. I've been doing nothing for years.
35. I bet you I could stop gambling.
36. I eat my tacos over a tortilla. That way when stuff falls out, BOOM, another taco.
37. I can't believe I got fired from the calendar factory. All I did was take a day off.
38. I married Miss Right. I just didn't know her first name was Always.
39. I wasn't originally going to get a brain transplant; but then I changed my mind.
40. The best things in life are free. * plus shipping and handling *
41. Cats spend two thirds of their lives sleeping, and the other third making viral videos.
42. Refusing to go to the gym counts as resistance training, right?
43. I saw a sign that said "Watch for children" and I thought, "That sounds like a fair trade."
44. Why do we bake cookies and cook bacon?
45. One day you're the best thing since sliced bread. The next, you're toast.
46. Accidentally pooped my pants in the elevator. I'm taking this crap to a whole new level.
47. TRUE FRIENDSHIP: Walking into a person's house and your Wi-Fi connects automatically.
48. People say money is not the key to happiness, but I always figured if you had enough money, you can have a key made.
49. Isn't it weird how when a cop drives by you feel paranoid instead of protected?
50. I knew my acne was really bad when a blind person tried reading my face.
51. I'm glad I know sign language, it's pretty handy.
52. I like birthdays, but I think too many can kill you.
53. I am on a seafood diet. Every time I see food, I eat it.
54. Every time I find the meaning of life, they change it.
55. Any room is a panic room if you've lost your phone in it.
56. Music makes every day better, especially if you turn it up just loud enough to drown out all the people around you.
57. I'm emotionally constipated. I haven't given a crap in days.
58. I was going to look for my missing watch, but I could never find the time.
59. A friend of mine tried to annoy me with bird puns, but I soon realized that toucan play at that game.
60. Studies have shown that most people who eat a lot are overweight. But these are just round figures.
61. I started a new band called 999 Megabyte. We haven't reached a gig yet!
62. Why do we wash bath towels? Aren't we clean when we use them?
63. Three tourists are driving down the highway trying to get to Disneyland. They saw a sign that read "Disneyland Left." So they went home.
64. If the Cincinnati Reds were really the first major-league baseball team, who did they play?
65. Did you know they had to bury president George Washington standing up because he could never lie?

66. At my old school, my teacher asked me if I knew Abraham Lincoln's Gettysburg Address. "Gettysburg?" I said. "I thought he lived in Washington."
67. There was a power outage at a department store yesterday. Twenty people were trapped on the escalators.
68. It was not school that Joe disliked; it was just the principal of it.
69. My wife is so negative. I remembered the car seat, the stroller, AND the diaper bag. Yet all she can talk about is how I forgot the baby!
70. I used to be in a band, we were called 'lost dog'. You probably saw our posters.
71. I childproofed the house... but they still get in!
72. I wondered why the Frisbee was getting bigger, and then it hit me.
73. I haven't spoken to my wife for 18 months- I don't like to interrupt her.
74. Parallel lines have so much in common. It's a shame they'll never meet.
75. My wife accused me of being immature. I told her to get out of my fort.
76. I called a psychic once. She asked me who was on the line, so I hung up.
77. Nothing political is correct.
78. Always remember you're unique, just like everyone else.
79. I get enough exercise just pushing my luck!
80. I don't approve of political jokes... I've seen to many of them get elected!
81. I am a nobody, nobody is perfect, therefore I am perfect.
82. Never argue with a fool. They will lower you to their level, and then beat you with experience.
83. Just changed my Facebook name to "No one" so when I see stupid posts I can click like and it will say, "No one likes this"!
84. Crime doesn't pay, does that mean my job is a crime?
85. I had a dream I was eating a giant marshmallow, when I woke up my pillow was missing!
86. Never iron a four leaf clover. You don't want to press your luck!
87. I bet the butcher $50 that he couldn't reach the meat on the top shelf. He said, "No, the steaks are too high."
88. Nothing ruins a Friday more than realizing that today is Tuesday!
89. Hard work never killed anybody, but why take a chance?
90. When a man tells you he got rich through hard work, ask him who's.
91. Failure is not an option- it comes bundled with the software.
92. I just torn up a notepad and wrapped it around my stomach; it was a waist of paper!
93. I've been trying to push the envelope at work, but it's still stationary.
94. If Apple made a car, would it have Windows?
95. My friend's bakery burned down last night. Now his business is toast.
96. My first job was working in an orange juice factory, but I got canned because I couldn't concentrate.
97. I used to be a banker, but I lost interest.
98. Two peanuts walk into a bar. One was a salted.
99. When an actress saw her first strands of gray hair, she thought she'd dye.

100. An invisible man marries an invisible woman. Their kids were nothing to look at either.
101. Never lie to an X-ray technician. They can see right through you.
102. To the guy who invented zero: Thanks for nothing.
103. I've been to the dentist several times, so I know the drill.
104. Time flies like an arrow. Fruit flies like a banana.
105. When you've seen one shopping center, you've seen a mall.
106. Be kind to your dentist. He has fillings too.
107. Jokes about German sausage are the wurst.
108. I couldn't work out how to fasten my seatbelt. Then it clicked.
109. We're going on a class trip to the Coca-Cola factory. I hope there's no pop quiz.
110. Women who wear $200 perfume obviously have no common scents.
111. Snoop Dog had a birthday today. When asked what it was like to get older, Snoop Dog, "Ruff.
112. When you get a bladder infection, urine trouble.
113. All the toilets in New York's police stations have been stolen. Now police have nothing to go on.
114. I used to be a baker, but I didn't make enough dough.
115. I hate insect puns, they really bug me.
116. A book just fell on my head. I've only got myshelf to blame.
117. Yesterday, a clown held the door open for me. I thought it was a nice jester.
118. Don't trust people who do acupuncture, they're back stabbers.
119. A new broom has came out. It is sweeping the nation.
120. The first time I got a universal remote control I thought to myself, "This changes everything."
121. My girlfriend asked me to stop impersonating a flamingo. I had to put my foot down.
122. I left my last girlfriend because she wouldn't stop counting. I wonder what she's up to now.
123. I love my time machine. Me and it go way back.
124. I can hear music coming out of the printer. I think the paper's jammin' again.
125. Getting paid to sleep would be a dream job.
126. I don't trust these stairs- they're always up to something.
127. I've on accidentally swallowed some Scrabble tiles. My next poop could spell disaster.
128. Someone just stole my mood ring. I'm not sure how I feel about it.
129. Inspecting mirrors is a job I could really see myself doing.
130. There was a big paddle sale at the boat store. It was quite an oar deal.
131. My grandma's having trouble with her new stair lift. It's driving her up the wall.
132. It was an emotional wedding. Even the cake was in tiers.
133. Singing in the shower is all fun and games until you get shampoo in your mouth. Then it becomes a soap opera.
134. If a judge loves the sound of his own voice, expect a long sentence.
135. I've been learning braille. I'm sure I'll master it once I get a feel for it.

136. I applied for a job at the local restaurant. I'm still waiting.

137. Broken puppets for sale. No strings attached.

138. I saw an advert that read: "Television for sale. $1, volume stuck on full." I thought to myself, "I can't turn that down."

139. I'm working on a device that will read minds. I'd love to hear your thoughts.

140. My friend made a joke about a TV controller. It wasn't remotely funny.

141. Sue broke her finger today, but on the other hand, she was completely fine.

142. I was struggling to figure out how lightning works, then it struck me.

143. Cross- country skiing is great- if you live in a small country.

144. I think cave people invented hockey in the Ice Age.

145. Teachers say our future depends on our dreams, but they never let us sleep in class.

146. My doctor gave me pills for my B.O. Unfortunately, they kept slipping out from under my arms!

147. I have a very frustrated pet at home. It's a turtle that loves to chase cars.

148. The food at the medical school cafeteria is so bad that with every meal you get a free prescription.

149. Did you ever wonder if milk comes out of a cow's nose when it laughs?

150. Two goldfish are in a tank. One says to the other, "Do you know how to drive this thing?"

151. A man with two left feet walks into a shoe shop and buys some flip flips.

152. I told my girlfriend she drew her eyebrows too high. She seemed surprised.

153. Pencil sharpeners have tough lives... They live off tips.

154. I used to work in a blanket factory, but it folded.

155. I used to be a shoe salesman, until they gave me the boot.

156. Two silk worms had a race. They ended up in a tie.

157. I hated my job as an origami teacher. There was too much paperwork!

158. I had a mole removed a few months ago. I really miss it. I miss it because it grew on me.

159. The other day, a man came to my front door asking for donations for the local swimming pool. So I gave him a small glass of water!

160. I wrote a song about a tortilla. It's actually more of a wrap.

161. Once I got angry at a chef at an Italian restaurant, so I gave him a pizza my mind.

162. I never wanted to believe that my Dad was stealing from his job as a road worker. But when I got home, all the signs were there.

163. I went to the bank the other day and asked the banker to check my balance, so she pushed me!

164. 20 years ago we had Johnny Cash, Bob Hope, and Steve Jobs. Now we have no Cash, no Hope, and no jobs. Please don't let Kevin Bacon die.

165. I predict that in the future, YouTube, Twitter, and Facebook will merge to create one super time-wasting site called YouTwitFace.

166. Someone stole my Microsoft Office and they're gonna pay! You have my word.

167. I used to be addicted to the hokey pokey, but then I turned myself around.

168. Whiteboards are remarkable.
169. At what age do you tell a highway it's adopted?
170. Why isn't there mouse-flavored cat food?
171. Why is a dog's nose always wet?
172. Circles are so pointless.
173. Are children who use sign language allowed to talk with their mouth full?
174. Why do they call him Donkey Kong if he is not a donkey?
175. Cartoonist found dead in home. Details are sketchy.
176. I just got hit by a rented car. It Hertz.
177. I know a lot of jokes about unemployed people- but none of them work.
178. If you are bald, what hair color do they put on your driver's license?
179. What happens if you get scared half to death twice?
180. My mom bought cheap toilet paper. Bad decision. Now we got a real mess on our hands.
181. One housewife had a kitchen so small that she could only have condensed milk.
182. "Mom! There's a man at the door collecting for the old folks' home. Shall I give him Grandma?"
183. A seminar on time travel will be held last Tuesday.
184. Black holes are most commonly found in black socks.
185. Entered what I ate today into my new fitness app and it just sent an ambulance to my house.
186. Turning vegan is a big missed steak.
187. People are a lot less judgy when you say you ate an 'avocado salad' instead of a bowl of guacamole.
188. The dinner I was cooking for my family was going to be a surprise but the fire trucks ruined it.
189. My annual performance review says I lack "passion and intensity", guess management hasn't seen me alone with a Big Mac.
190. I got fired from my job as a chef for stealing kitchen equipment. It's a whisk I was willing to take.
191. Cannibals like to meat people.
192. I went to a peanut factory last week. It was nuts!
193. Subway is definitely the healthiest fast food available because they make you get out of the car.
194. eBay is so useless. I tried to look up lighters and all they had was 13,749 matches.
195. I wanna make a joke about sodium, but Na.
196. I saw an ad for burial plots, and thought to myself, "This is the last thing I need."
197. A bus station is where a bus stops. A train station is where a train stops. On my desk, I have a work station.
198. I found a rock yesterday which measured 1,760 yards in length. Must be some kind of milestone.
199. I'm taking part in a stair climbing competition. Guess I better step up my game.

200. Why is the man who invests all your money called a broker?
201. Turtles think frogs are homeless.
202. My email password has been hacked again. That's the third time I've had to rename the cat.
203. The good Lord didn't create anything without a purpose, but mosquitoes came close.
204. I've always had a hard time with decimals, I just don't see the point.
205. If we breathe oxygen in the daytime, do we breathe nitrogen when we're asleep?
206. I have a fear of negative numbers. I will stop at nothing to avoid them.
207. Two mysterious people live in my house. Somebody and Nobody. Somebody did it and Nobody knows who.
208. Just had a rant in which I said I hope the entire world explodes tomorrow. Probably went too far. Sorry for including you all.
209. Don't steal. That's the government's job.
210. If my iPod doesn't work in the next few minutes, I'm throwing it in the river. It can either sync or swim.
211. Panic attack: When you don't feel your phone in your pocket.
212. Calendars? Their days are numbered.
213. My parents always told me I could be anyone I wanted and now I've been charged with identity theft. Parents cannot be trusted.
214. I'm making a TV show about hijacking a plane. We just shot the pilot.
215. I love watching The Simpsons. They never get old.
216. My cooking is so awesome, even the smoke alarm cheers me on.
217. You don't have to be crazy to work here. We'll train you.
218. I remember when yoga was called Twister.
219. Butterflies aren't what they used to be.
220. When I die, I'm going to have 'free WiFi' written on my tombstone. That way, more people will visit.
221. A bargain is something you don't need at a price you can't resist.
222. I find mind-readers really annoying, and I bet they don't even know why.
223. A mime will never give you bad advice.
224. Fun fact: MC Hammer wrote 'U Can't Touch This' when he worked in a museum.
225. I find a duck's opinion of me is very much influenced by whether or not I have bread.
226. I order the club sandwich all the time and I'm not even a member. I don't know how I get away with it.
227. Success is like a fart. It only bothers people when it's not their own.
228. Sunrises are just as beautiful as sunsets only less crowded.
229. I just ran into one of the Seven Dwarfs. He wasn't Happy.
230. I broke up with my gym. We were just not working out.
231. I always start my diet on the same day...tomorrow.
232. It's not the fall that kills you. It's the sudden stop at the end.
233. When I'm depressed, I cut myself...a piece of cake.
234. I've got a wife who never misses me. Her aim is perfect.

235. My brother and I laugh at how competitive we were as kids. But I laugh more.
236. I tried to daydream, but my mind kept wandering.
237. If you think you aren't creative, buy a gym membership and see how many excuses you find not to use it.
238. The people who talked about me behind my back discussed me.
239. I went window shopping today. I bought 4 windows.
240. I do charity work. I volunteer my opinion just about every day.
241. When I said I wanted to live life in the fast lane, I didn't mean the one with oncoming traffic.
242. I got my hair highlighted, because I felt some strands were more important than others.
243. I honestly enjoy long romantic walks to the fridge.
244. A clean desk is the sign of a new employee.
245. Deep down, I knew scuba diving wasn't for me.
246. Short in the front, long in the back... Pick-up trucks are the mullets of automobiles.
247. Just reported a zookeeper for completely ignoring the ' Do Not Feed the Animals' sign.
248. This match won't light. Which is weird, because it did this morning.
249. I can't help being lazy. It walks in the family.
250. The recipe said 'set the oven to 180 degrees', so I did, but now I can't open it because the door faces the wall.
251. I've owned three golden retrievers and not once has one of them brought me any gold.
252. I can only imagine how I'd look in a blindfold.
253. I don't like my hands. I always keep them at arm's length.
254. I hate people who say 'age is just a number'- age is clearly a word.
255. I slept like a log last night. I woke up in a fireplace.
256. My wife does really good bird imitations. She watches me like a hawk.
257. I bought my wife some of that 'volume control' shampoo. Doesn't work, I can still hear her.
258. I can keep secrets, it's the people I tell who can't.
259. My brain is giving me the silent treatment today.
260. Sky News would be a great name for a weather channel.
261. Getting a job repairing revolving doors was a real turning point in my life.
262. Sometimes I wrap myself in bows and call myself gifted.
263. Vampires are a real pain in the neck.
264. A burrito is a sleeping bag for ground beef.
265. I need a six-month holiday, twice a year.
266. My friend just called me saying they've had their first child, 8lb, 2oz. Stupid name for a baby if you ask me.
267. If Barbie is so popular, then why do you have to buy her friends?
268. I slept like a baby last night. Woke up every two hours screaming.
269. I was taught how to get on planes at boarding school.

270. The Energizer Bunny got arrested. He was charged with battery.

271. The trouble with jogging is, by the time you realize you're not in shape, it's too far to walk back.

272. I don't just have issues; I have a subscription.

273. I threw some snow at my wife but she didn't catch my drift.

274. Cashiers are always checking me out.

275. E-flat walks into a bar. The bartender says, " Sorry, we don't serve minors."

276. A termite walks into a bar and says, " Is the bartender here?"

277. It was my son's birthday so I decided to take four of his friends to McDonald's and then bowling. They had a great time, he would've loved it.

278. Life's too short to get you many points in Scrabble.

279. When it comes to a battle with words I'm always ready to mumble.

280. FedEx and UPS are merging. There new company will be called FedUp.

281. Dieting is wishful shrinking.

282. I'm working out right now. I'm exercising my eyebrow muscles by raising them high. Try it; you'll be surprised.

283. My belt holds my trousers up, but the belt loops hold my belt up- so which one's the real hero?

284. I stepped on a cornflake. Now I'm a cereal killer.

285. After looking at my bank account, it's time for me to make some tough decisions. Anyone want to buy some Pokémon cards?

286. I'm so good at sleeping I can even do it with my eyes closed.

287. I got into skinny jeans for a little while but I just couldn't pull them off.

288. If I eat healthy today then I can have one chocolate as a reward. If I eat unhealthy, I can have the whole box.

289. I have a large seashell collection, which I keep scattered on beaches all over the world.

290. I get all my tattoos done for free because I'm an identical twin. I just send my brother back for a refund.

291. I am the author of my life. Unfortunately, I'm writing in pen and I can't erase my mistakes.

292. As a kid I was made to walk the plank. We couldn't afford a dog.

293. My assistant is out today. Anyone know how to do everything?

294. A guy walks into a pub with a lump of asphalt on his shoulder. He says to the barman, " Give us a pint and one for the road."

295. I've just won the 'Most Secretive Person 2017' award... I can't tell you how much it means to me.

296. One, three, five, seven, nine and eleven kicked the crap out of two and four. Two and four did not stand a chance because they were fighting against the odds.

297. Whoever said "Don't cry over spilt milk' hasn't seen the price of food lately.

298. My spiritual home has been repossessed.

299. There must be a secret slot in my dryer that makes all my socks disappear.

300. I'm sending out spam emails about diet pills, hoping to reach a wider audience.
301. I think my eyesight's fine, but my judge disagrees. He says I need supervision.
302. My wife plays the piano by ear. Sometimes her earrings get in the way.
303. I still think Barack Obama stole 'Yes We Can' from Bob the Builder.
304. I bought a book on obedience seven years ago, but it turns out the dog is a slow reader.
305. I'd hate to be a giraffe with a sore throat.
306. Just gave two slices of bread a two minute makeover in the toaster and they've popped back up looking HOT!
307. I don't understand why people sob quietly. Use a megaphone for crying out loud.
308. I think animal testing is a terrible idea; they get all nervous and give the wrong answers.
309. It's so sad that birthday cakes don't live long enough to have birthdays of their own.
310. Chickens don't have friends. They just have pen pals.
311. I don't think I could ever stab someone. I mean, let's be honest. I can barely get the straw through the Capri Sun.
312. I had the right to remain silent, but I didn't have the ability too.
313. When I was born, I was so shocked I didn't talk for a year and a half.
314. Intelligence is like underwear. It's important that you have it but there's no need to show it off.
315. I don't have a problem with caffeine. I have a problem without caffeine.
316. I bought my wife a wooden leg for Christmas. It wasn't her main present, just a stocking stuffer.
317. I could snap at any moment. Seriously, with either hand.
318. Having Barack Obama's initials must stink.
319. I hate it when you call shotgun but the cops still throw you in the back.
320. I heard there was a new store called Moderation. They have everything there.
321. I went to a book store and asked the saleswoman where the Self Help section was, she said if she told me it would defeat the purpose.
322. I cut my finger chopping cheese, but I think that I may have grater problems.
323. My cat was just sick on the carpet. I don't think its feline well.
324. I dreamed about drowning in an ocean made of orange soda last night. It took me a while to work out it was just a Fanta sea.
325. I needed a password eight characters long so I picked 'Snow White and the Seven Dwarfs.
326. I am terrified of elevators. I'm going to start taking steps to avoid them.
327. Last night me and my girlfriend watched three DVD's back to back. Luckily I was the one facing the TV.
328. Atheism is a non-prophet organization.
329. Just watched a documentary about beavers... it was the best damn program I've ever seen.
330. They laughed when I said I wanted to be a comedian- they're not laughing now.

331. A police officer caught two kids playing with a car battery and a firework. He charged one and let the other one off.

332. I'm reading a book on the history of glue- can't put it down.

333. I went to the zoo the other day, there was only one dog in it. It was a shitzu.

334. As a musician, I hate the key of E minor. It gives me the E-B-G-B's.

335. I did an exam about marriage today. I answered every question with 'The Wife' and failed. Turns out she's not always right.

336. My wife is a great lover... of cakes.

337. I thought I'd forgotten how to play Tetris, but once I started all the pieces seemed to fall into place.

338. I went to an Italian restaurant, and they had spaghetti on the menu. So I had to call the waiter to wipe it off.

339. I had a wet dream last night. I fell asleep in the bath.

340. Sometimes I watch football holding an Xbox controller just to screw with my mom's head.

341. I wanted to propose to my girlfriend over the phone. So I gave her a ring.

342. I was in the gym earlier and I decided to jump on the treadmill. People were giving me weird looks, so I started jogging instead.

343. Past, Present, and Future walked into a bar. It was tense.

344. My grandma suffers from Alzheimer's. It's her birthday next week, so I bought her a memory card.

345. Exercise bikes get you nowhere.

346. I was going to buy a book on phobias, but I was afraid it wouldn't help me.

347. Time to get a new fitness plan. The old one wasn't working out.

348. Sometimes I enjoy my steak undercooked, but that's rare.

349. Why do fat chance and slim chance mean the same thing?

350. A friend of mine said he wanted to improve his golf. I suggested that he should go on a course.

351. A detective I know dropped his iPhone today. He cracked the case.

352. If you're using public transport, never give up your seat to an old lady. That's how my uncle lost his job as a bus driver.

353. Not impressed by these so-called long-life light bulbs. We kitted out Granddad's whole house with them and he still died.

354. As my late father always said, get a decent watch.

355. Fox is so twentieth century.

356. I miss my umbilical cord. I grew attached to it.

357. Dear Student Loans, Thank you for saving my life. I can't think how I can ever repay you.

358. I just read a list of '100 things to do before you die'. I'm pretty surprised 'yell for help' wasn't one of them.

359. Someone once told me that the camera adds 10lbs. Which is why I didn't pack it in my suitcase.

360. So Apple is making an announcement tonight. Maybe they're going to merge with Blackberry and launch their new 'Crumble'.

361. My doctor told me that I had to give up drinking. It's been three days now and I feel really dehydrated!

362. People call me Mr. Compromise. It wasn't my first choice for a nickname, but I can live with it.

363. The supermarket has stopped selling tropical fruit. It's enough to make a mango crazy.

364. My friends say I'll believe anything. Damn, I suppose they're right.

365. How long a minute depends on what side of the bathroom door you're on.

366. My wife kicked me out so I've been living in a telephone booth. I just wanted somewhere to call home.

367. I saved loads of cash on the new iPhone yesterday. I didn't buy one.

368. I just saw a beautiful girl with a massive gut. What a waist.

369. I told a volcano joke down at the pub last night. The whole place erupted.

370. 'Coming soon to a cinema near you'... How do they know where I live?

371. Last week the candle factory burned down. Everyone just stood around and sang ' Happy Birthday'.

372. I don't know why I just bought some new coconut shampoo... I haven't even got any coconuts.

373. It pains me to say it, but I have a sore throat.

374. Everybody says stealing is wrong. Personally I don't buy it.

375. I am going to make some felt pens. Does anyone have any tips?

376. It's never too late to start. Which is why I'm putting it off till tomorrow.

377. A train driver's job is pretty straight forward.

378. When I walked into the shop, the sign on the door said 'Open'. Now I can't leave because it says 'Closed'.

379. I watched a documentary about pigs last night. I thought they were pretty boring animals, but it turns out there's a twist in the tail.

380. I've been sent to jail for procrastinating. I'll finish my sentence next month.

381. My wife accused me of being a terrible lawyer. I couldn't defend myself.

382. Major car collision at Spaghetti Junction: twelve injured, four pasta way.

383. I think my wife said I'm never certain about anything.

384. How to make Easter easier: replace the 't' with an 'I'.

385. Me and my recliner go way back.

386. I was just about to nail some shelves to the wall. Then I thought, screw it.

387. I've made a product that increases the size of your basement. I hope it'll be a big cellar.

388. Coffee is not my cup of tea.

389. My wife left me because of my obsession with Africa. Kenya believe that?

390. I had an ice-cube fight last night. It didn't last long; things got a bit heated.

391. My wife just left me for Arnold Schwarzenegger... she'll be back.

392. Reincarnation is making a comeback.

393. I'm a terrible psychic- I don't know about you.
394. To people who hate hand gestures: I salute you.
395. Two rights don't make a wrong. They make a U-turn.
396. My wife's leaving me because I never take her seriously. It's ok though, she'll be back tomorrow.
397. My friends say my geology jokes are lame, but I think they rock.
398. I just won't stand for people who try to take my seat.
399. I've just made some origami Teenage Mutant Ninja Turtles. Now watch them as they face their greatest foe: Shredder.
400. I'm mad because my friends say I'm a terrible mind-reader. What are your thoughts.
401. My wife left me because of my obsession with Scrabble. Obsession: eleven points.
402. I have a spider on my keyboard. It's ok though, I have it under Ctrl.
403. I broke my leg and the doctor said he's going to have to put me in a cast. How does he expect me to sing and dance in this condition,
404. If you throw a cat out of the car window, does it become kitty litter?
405. Don't you hate it when Wikipedia copies your homework?
406. My wife's leaving me as I'm too controlling. It's ok though, I'm not letting her.
407. I'm not a competitive person... I'll be the first to admit it.
408. My wife's so lazy our smoke alarm has a snooze button.
409. I can't say I've ever seen anyone were camouflage before.
410. I hate having to brush my teeth every morning. I must be the only person in the world with hairy teeth.
411. I just got a new aftershave that smells like breadcrumbs. The birds love it.
412. I don't like grudges. My father kept grudges. I always hated him for it.
413. What if I never learn how to use rhetorical questions?
414. When my wife and I got married, she treated me like a god. As time went by, the letters got reversed.
415. My girlfriend thinks I have a gambling addiction. She hasn't said anything, but I bet that's what she's thinking.
416. I read something the other day that made me piss myself. It was a sign that said ' Bathroom's closed'.
417. My wife left me because I'm not very approachable. It was the harshest email I ever got.
418. I think I'm going to order a load of bubble wrap, just to see what it's delivered in.
419. My New Year's resolution is to save enough money to buy a Velcro wall. And I plan on sticking to it.
420. Somebody threw some cheese at me the other day. I thought to myself 'How dairy?'
421. There's a fine line between a numerator and a denominator.
422. I'm the kind of guy who stops the microwave with one second to go, just to feel like a bomb diffuser.
423. Is there a difference between well done and done well?
424. I invented gloves. Ok, I'm lying, but I did have a hand in it.

425. If snow is made of water and water has no calories, how come snowmen are fat?

426. Has anyone pointed out to Americans that the 'gas' they're putting in their cars is a liquid?

427. People often accuse me of lying… they don't really, I made that up.

428. I work as a waiter. The pay isn't great, but I put food on the table.

429. I've just put my clock backwards. It didn't help at all, I can't see the time now.

430. I felt quite smug when the iPad came out. I'd been saying for years that the iPhone would be big one day.

431. I gave blood today. I know it's not the best gift to give my wife for Valentine's Day, but it came from the heart.

432. My ex-wife says it was my obsession Taurus apart.

433. My uncle was so stubborn, when he died he left a won't.

434. A little birdie told me my golf skills are improving.

435. If vegetarians love animals so much, why do they eat all their food.

436. Smoke detectors need to be tested from time to time. So sometimes I cook something.

437. If you would like to help with the restoration of our local jeweler's shop, please give us a ring.

438. My eyelids are so sexy I can't keep my eyes off them.

439. A few weeks ago, two cartoonists entered a contest. The result was a draw.

440. My new band is called 'Deaf' … we've just been signed.

441. I need to find my aim in life before I run out of ammunition.

442. My girlfriend told me she was seeing someone else behind my back. I don't know how, I was sitting against a wall.

443. I've done 100 pull-ups today. This new belt is terrible.

444. Has anyone else noticed that mirrors look really sexy?

445. I miss my wife's cooking… every chance I get.

446. I think my smartphone is broken. I pressed the home button but I'm still at work.

447. I just got fired from my job at the Psychic Hotline. Didn't see that coming.

448. Whenever I go near a book, I get withdrawal symptoms.

449. I hate being bipolar. It's amazing.

450. I always refuse to cut corners. Which is why I lost my job as a carpenter.

451. If people were meant to pop out of bed first thing in the morning, we'd all sleep in toasters.

452. I used to know this guy that hung around the corner of maps. He was a legend.

453. If we aren't supposed to eat animals, then why are they made out of meat?

454. Though many people think the letter 'M' is quite common, it actually only occurs once in a blue moon.

455. Never hit a man with glasses. Hit him with a baseball bat.

456. I gave a pint of blood yesterday. I hate mosquito season.

457. I think hitchhikers are really friendly. I've gone past three in the last hour and they all gave me the thumbs up.

458. The Insomnia Olympics- you snooze, you lose.
459. Whenever I'm sad, I try to imagine a T-Rex trying to put on a hat.
460. Birthdays are good for you. Statistics show that the people who have the most live the longest.
461. My doctor said I need to quit my helium addiction before I get carried away.
462. I want to go into a balloon store and threaten to blow the whole place up!
463. I have a phone interview tomorrow. What are some good questions to ask a phone?
464. If a deaf person swears, does his mother wash his hands with soap?
465. I have a hidden talent... I wish I could find it.
466. I'll bet wild hogs tell boaring stories.
467. My wife says she's going to leave me for being too impatient. I can't wait.
468. The last time someone told me I looked hot it was 102 degrees outside.
469. My dog has been sitting outside in front of the snowman for an hour, waiting for it to throw one of those twigs.
470. No matter how loud car alarms are, cars never seem to wake up.
471. A magician was driving down the road. Then he turned into a driveway.
472. As I sat there licking my guitar, I thought to myself, ' I have a good taste in music.'
473. I don't want to get carried away here, but these security guards aren't really giving me a choice.
474. This next song is 'Subtraction'. Take it away!
475. You always remember your first crush. Mine was orange.
476. Constipated people don't give a crap.
477. The love between two mimes is unspoken love.
478. Watch repairmen always get to work on time.
479. I never use body butter. I don't want to make myself irresistible to cannibals.
480. I dedicate this show to my dad who was a roofer. So Dad, if you're up there...
481. Unfortunately, putting a bow on your head does not make you gifted.
482. Whatever you do in life, give 100 percent... unless you're donating blood.
483. I love my six-pack. That's why I protect it with a thick layer of fat.
484. Does running away from your problems count as exercising?
485. I've done a close-up sketch of a fish. It's a scale drawing.
486. I'm surprised that the hip-hop culture hasn't caught on with rabbits.
487. If I could be any person, living or dead, I'd definitely be a living person.
488. Is there another word for synonym?
489. Is reading in the bathroom considered multi-tasking?
490. I'm not getting old. I'm becoming a classic.
491. The doctor told me I suffer with insomnia. I stayed awake all night worrying about it.
492. If a pope goes to the bathroom, is it considered holy crap?
493. Just told my joke about Peter Pan again. Never gets old.
494. I just phoned the police because someone broke into my home and released thousands of house flies in it. They're sending out the swat team.

495. Wanted: person to inflate balloons. The ideal candidate knows how to blow things out of proportion.
496. Why is it called tourist season if we can't shoot them?
497. I'm not lazy, I'm energy efficient.
498. The road to ADHD is paved with bad attentions.
499. On a scale of nine to ten, how would you rate me?
500. An advert begs me to try 'the toothbrush most dental professionals use' and I think, 'That's gross; I'll buy my own.'
501. Say what you want about drunk people, but at least they've had all their shots.
502. The favorite music of Irish teenagers is sham-rock.
503. I hate when people say, 'Here's a picture of me when I was younger.' Isn't every picture of you when you were younger?
504. Photons have mass? I didn't even know they were Catholic.
505. Butterflies are not what they used to be.
506. My wife left me because she said I'm addicted to oxymoron's. She was pretty ugly anyways.
507. Recent research has shown that six out of seven dwarves aren't happy.
508. I've gained twenty pounds of belly fat since I landed a desk job. I think of it as my industrial waist.
509. Remember, there are two words in life that will open a lot of doors for you. 'Push' and 'pull'.
510. The inventor of the ballet skirt was struggling for a name, until he finally put tu and tu together.
511. How come no supervillain has ever tried to kill Spiderman with insect repellent?
512. I always keep my chin up. If I don't, people might find out that I have more than one.
513. I have no idea why I walked into the short-term memory clinic.
514. One thing I know about the speed of light is it always gets here way too early in the morning.
515. Recipes are like online dating websites. They never end up looking like the picture.
516. I try not to limit my madness to March.
517. Breaking news: 'The Kodak Film company has filed for bankruptcy.' More details to come as the story develops.
518. I'm calling it a night... because it's dark outside.
519. Bathroom forecast- Good chance of showers today.
520. My wife left me because of my obsession with glass. I'm shattered.
521. Robots are never anxious. They have nerves of steel.
522. Warnings are so stupid. Like on this deodorant: 'Avoid contact with eyes.' Too late, I've already seen it.
523. You can't fire me, I'm not even loaded.
524. Do mimes observe a brief moment of talking when a fellow mime passes away?
525. I wanted to be a farmer at one time, but it turned out to be the wrong field for me.
526. I respect giraffes, but I always get the impression they're looking down on me.

527. A really hot girl asked me for my number today and all I had to do was hit her car with my car.
528. It's like these advertisers know what I want even before I do!
529. Roosters are just edible alarm clock.
530. My body is less beefcake and more cheesecake.
531. The great thing about gingerbread men is that each one is a new chance to bite somebody's head off.
532. Calories make the world go round.
533. Life is like a hot bath: It feels good while you're in it, but the longer you stay, the more wrinkled you get.
534. Four out of five bubble baths result in Santa Claus beards.
535. The sole purpose of a child's middle name is so he can tell when he's really in trouble.
536. I need a job sleeping, with lots of overtime.
537. Hundreds of kids are shipped off to mime boarding school every year, never to be heard from again.
538. I only make mental bets. And, coincidentally, I've lost my mind.
539. "Goodnight honey", I said as I got up to go to bed. I'm trying to make the marmalade jealous.
540. Once in a while I take the blame when the dog farts, just to repay him.
541. If a man said he'll fix it, he will. There's no need to remind him about it every six months.
542. Sleep is at the top of my list of places I'd like to go back to.
543. My first stand-up attempt was a disaster. Mind you I was only ten months old at the time.
544. If you leave alphabet soup on the stove unattended, it could spell disaster.
545. You can learn many things from children. How much patience you have, for example.
546. If actions speak louder than words, why can't we hear mimes?
547. My wife has finally left me because of my history obsession, even though I told her that it's all in the past.
548. If those NASA scientists were so smart, how come they all counted backwards?
549. My girlfriend said she's tired of my obsession with martial arts. So I kicked her out.
550. Musicians are always getting themselves into treble.
551. I slept like a rock last night. I woke up in a flower bed.
552. Beware when taking a magician's exam: the test is loaded with trick questions.
553. This orange juice says concentrate, but it doesn't say for how long.
554. I don't know what my deal with gum is. I guess it kind of stuck with me.
555. Apple pie isn't American unless you eat the whole thing in one sitting.
556. Keep the dream alive: Hit the snooze button.
557. My friend keeps trying to convince me that he's a compulsive liar but I don't believe him.
558. My friend keeps trying to convince me that he's a compulsive liar but I don't believe him.

559. I recently decided to sell my vacuum cleaner as all it was doing was gathering dust.

560. Some people are like Slinkies … not really good for anything, but you can't help smiling when you see one tumble down the stairs.

561. The sole purpose of a child's middle name, is so he can tell when he's really in trouble.

562. Crowded elevators smell different to midgets.

563. Whenever I fill out an application, in the part that says "If an emergency, notify:" I put "DOCTOR". What's my mother going to do?

564. I intend to live forever. So far, so good.

565. I used to be indecisive. Now I'm not sure.

566. I like work. It fascinates me. I sit and look at it for hours.

567. The difference between an oral thermometer and a rectal thermometer is in the taste.

568. It is hard to understand how a cemetery raised its burial cost and blamed it on the cost of living.

569. The Miss Universe pageant is fixed. All the winners are from Earth.

570. No one is listening until you fart.

571. I wanna hang a map of the world in my house. Then I'm gonna put pins into all the locations that I've traveled to. But first, I'm gonna have to travel to the top two corners of the map so it won't fall down.

572. Ham and Eggs: A day's work for a chicken, a lifetime commitment for a pig.

573. Don't hate me because I'm handsome. Hate me because your girlfriend thinks so.

574. My room isn't dirty, I just have everything on display.

575. Relationships are like farting, if you push too hard, things could get messy real fast.

576. Why is "abbreviated" such a long word?

577. Friendship is like peeing your pants. Everyone can see it, but only you can truly feel it's warmth.

578. If God wanted us to be thin, food wouldn't taste so good.

579. When I asked my wife what she wanted for her birthday she said 'Just gimme something with diamonds.' That's why I got her a pack of cards.

580. My doctor told me to watch my drinking. Now I drink in front of a mirror.

581. I accidentally pooped my pants in the elevator. I guess I'm taking this shit to a whole new level.

582. I named my dog "5 miles", so I can tell people I walk 5 miles every day.

583. Shout out to my fingers, I can always count on them.

584. I love how people say they're "expecting" a baby, as if it might be something else, like a penguin.

585. I just saw an Apple store get robbed... does that make me an iWitness?

586. Today I bought cupcakes without sprinkles. Diets are hard.

587. I'm on the 'start tomorrow' diet.

588. Why do they call it multiple choice when you only get to pick one?

589. I like to keep my girlfriend on her toes. So I've been teaching her ballet.

590. Why do dogs always think the knock at the door is for them?

591. If we're not supposed to have pillow fights, why do they call them throw pillows?

592. Mountain climbers are curious types. They always want to take another peak.
593. I walked past a shop that was selling microscopes. So I went in for a closer look.
594. I decided to write a joke about restraining orders. This is the closest I could get.
595. A coffin? That's the last thing I need!
596. I couldn't pull out of my parking space. I had to use my back-up plan.
597. It's bad luck to be superstitions.
598. My internet went down. By which I mean, my neighbors changed their password.
599. "I live life on the edge." – Humpty Dumpty
600. Anyone can get old: all you have to do is live long enough.
601. After Monday and Tuesday, even the calendar is like W T F.
602. Chewbacca just did something wrong; total Wookie mistake.
603. Some things are best kept between you and the neighbors. Like a fence, for example.
604. I used to be afraid of the dark. Now I'm terrified of the electricity bill.
605. Pronouns: Like normal nouns, just highly trained.
606. There are only two levels in lion taming: 'expert' and 'cat food'.
607. I am yet to bite a moose that tastes like chocolate.
608. I just checked the height/weight chart at the gym. Apparently I'm four inches too short.
609. Coal diggers would probably make more money if they could mine their own business.
610. When you choke a Smurf, what color does it turn?
611. I used to work at a recycling plant. My job was to crush cans. It was soda pressing.
612. Who invented the brush they put next to the toilet? That thing hurts.
613. I've quit my new job as a postman. They handed me my first letter to deliver, I looked at it and thought: 'This isn't for me.'
614. I'm not allowed on cruise ships ever since that whole 'poop deck' misunderstanding.
615. Hearing aid for sale. Give me a shout if you're interested.
616. Guys think every girl's dream is to meet the perfect guy. Every girl's dream is to eat without getting fat.
617. Why is it so hard to find an exercise bike with a nice little basket where I can put my nachos?
618. I have a black eye in karate.
619. My wife spends hours in the bathroom teasing her hair. She's a blonde, so I doubt her hair gets her jokes.
620. The voices in my head may not be real, but they have some pretty good ideas.
621. I don't think all those screwdrivers really belong to Phillip.
622. Yesterday, my new girlfriend and I went on a date to the skating rink, but we were kicked out. We had started to break the ice.
623. "Have I made myself clear?" said the chameleon as he stood in front of a sheet of glass.
624. When I was six my family moved to a new city, but fortunately I was able to track them down.
625. I roasted a duck last night, but I don't think he got the jokes.

626. A Smurf walks into a bar. The bartender says, “Why so blue?”
627. I really like left-handed gloves. Although, on the other hand, I don’t.
628. Baby snakes probably throw a lot of hissy fits.
629. I’m at the age where I need to start watching what I eat, so I spend a lot of time looking at food.
630. You’d think the self-checkout lanes would have more mirrors.
631. My contacts have really been bothering me lately. So I deleted them from my phone.
632. I have an on-again off-again relationship with clothes.
633. If I were an accountant, I’d call myself The Thought. My slogan would be, ‘It’s the thought that counts.’
634. It’s easy to distract fat people. Piece of cake.
635. I never run with scissors. Actually, those last two words were unnecessary.
636. If there’s one thing I can’t stand, it’s up.
637. I’m so broke, I can’t even pay attention.
638. I can’t go to spelling competitions. I’m allergic to bees.
639. I miss my bus every morning. I never realized how attached we’d become until I bought my car.
640. I do ten sit-ups every morning. It might not sound like much, but there are only so many times you can hit the snooze button.
641. Recipe calls for a quarter cup of thyme. That’s fifteen minutes, right?
642. Shooting for the stars really is a waste of bullets.
643. Lifestyle tip: The best way to avoid parking tickets is to remove your windshield wipers.
644. There may be no excuse for laziness, but I’m still looking.
645. When I want to hide money from my wife, I put it with her keys.
646. In a restaurant window- ‘Eat now, pay waiter.’
647. I’d go to the gym more often, but I can never find a parking space near the front door.
648. Shouldn’t the air and space museum be empty?
649. Computer tablets are hard to swallow.
650. Why do they use sterilized needles for death by lethal injections?
651. “All my friends can see right through me.”- Casper the Ghost.
652. A human cannonball can’t quit before he’s fired.
653. You and I are best friends. Always remember that I will pick you up if you fall. Right after I stop laughing.
654. Hey, if anyone knows how to fix some broken hinges, my door’s always open.
655. People who use selfie sticks really need to have a good, long look at themselves.
656. When I was younger I felt like a man trapped inside a woman’s body. Then I was born.
657. I’m learning the hokey pokey. Not all of it. But – I’ve got the ins and outs.
658. Money can’t buy you happiness? Well, check this out, I bought myself a Happy Meal.
659. I can handle pain until it hurts.
660. I just let my mind wander, and it didn’t come back.

661. I won $3 million on the lottery this weekend so I decided to donate a quarter of it to charity. Now I have $2,999,999.75.
662. With great power, comes great electricity bills.
663. Dwarfs and midgets have very little in common.
664. When everything's coming your way, you're in the wrong lane.
665. I heard a great joke about amnesia but I forgot it.
666. Love may be blind, but marriage is a real eye-opener.
667. I used to have winter fat but now I have spring rolls.
668. As long as there are tests, there will be prayer in schools.
669. You kill vegetarian vampires with a steak to the heart.
670. I never forget a face, but in your case I'd be glad to make an exception.
671. I, for one, like Roman numerals.
672. I have a parrot and it talks. But it did not say it was hungry, so it died.
673. A big shout out to sidewalks... Thanks for keeping me off the streets.
674. Whatever you do in life, always give 100%. Unless you're donating blood.
675. I named my dog "5 miles" so I can tell people I walk 5 miles every day.
676. I had to quit my job at the shoe recycling factory. It was just sole destroying.
677. There are two rules for success: 1.) Don't tell all you know.
678. Do not touch, must be the scariest thing to read in Braille!
679. I have a fear of German sausages! Yes, I fear the wurst!
680. I invented a new word! Plagiarism!
681. My recliner and I - we go way back!
682. I thought I wanted a career, turns out I just wanted paychecks.
683. I have a joke about a cat... Just kitt'en.
684. If you ate pasta and antipasta, would you still be hungry?
685. Why do they report power outages on TV?
686. Is there another word for synonym?
687. When a man has a birthday, he takes a day off. When a woman has a birthday, she takes at least three years off.
688. It's bad luck to be superstitious.
689. Last week the candle factory burned down. Everyone just stood around and sang Happy Birthday.
690. What do batteries run on?
691. If you were going to shoot a mime, would you use a silencer?
692. If you saw a heat wave, would you wave back?
693. How young can you die of old age?
694. After they make styrofoam, what do they ship it in?
695. I used to work in a fire hydrant factory. You couldn't park anywhere near the place.
696. It's a good thing we have gravity, or else when birds died they'd just stay right up there. Hunters would be all confused.
697. I tried to draw my shadow once, but I couldn't... My arm kept moving.

698. People say that Disneyland is the happiest place on earth. Apparently, none of them have ever been in your arms.
699. I'm lost. Can you tell me which road leads to your heart?
700. My friend is so dumb, the pizza delivery guy asked him if he wanted his pizza cut into six slices or twelve. He said, "Cut it into six, I'm on a diet."
701. When cheese has its picture taken, what does it say?
702. If I melt enough dry ice, can I take a bath without getting wet?
703. Tips: They're like hugs, but without the awkward body contact.
704. I would tell you a chemistry joke, but all the good ones argon.
705. I would be willing to have almost any super power, but I can't see myself being invisible.
706. I need an insensitive joke to tell my deaf friend. Preferably one he's never heard.
707. If a musician plays baseball and they strike someone out, does that mean they have the perfect pitch?
708. I knew how to relieve my itchiness from scratch.
709. The idea of unsalted almonds is just plain nuts.
710. I chose to ignore my doctor when he told me I've got selective hearing.
711. I would shave my moustache, but it's really growing on me.
712. I'm holding a bubble wrap party. Feel free to pop in sometime.
713. Water, that's what floats my boat!
714. I hate peer pressure, and you should too.
715. Working as a plumber must be draining.
716. I'm a little short on midget jokes.
717. I don't understand speech bubbles, they go right over my head.
718. I lift weights as a hobby. At first, it was not easy to pick up.
719. I've bent over backwards trying to teach people limbo.
720. The closest I've ever gotten to a food diary is my shirt at the end of the day.
721. Do vegetarians eat animal crackers?
722. Installing car mufflers is an exhausting job.
723. Does Peter Pan peanut butter ever get old?
724. I beat my wife up this morning. She got up at seven and I got up at six.
725. I took a pen from the bank. It was off the chain.
726. I don't like it when my cab driver goes the extra mile for me.
727. Any bug can hit the windshield, but it takes guts to stick.
728. A day without sunshine is like, night.
729. The frustrated cannibal threw up his arms.
730. I'm looking at my ceiling- not saying it's the greatest ceiling in the world... but it's up there.
731. I moisturize my hair under one condition.
732. Power buttons are an instant turn on for me.
733. I can't count how many times I failed math.
734. I used to be shy, but since I've started rock climbing, I feel boulder.

735. I can always tell when they use fake dinosaurs in movies.
736. Whenever someone says they had a brain fart, I wonder if I can smell their farts.
737. In a week or so, I'm going to stop procrastinating.
738. I tried to steal a beverage, but it wasn't my cup of tea.
739. The oddest years of my high school career were 9th and 11th grade.
740. I was going to take Jonathan's place on the debate team, but he talked me out of it.
741. The shovel was a groundbreaking invention.
742. My friend offered to buy me a coffin, but I told him that's the last thing I'll need.
743. When deaf people fight, they let their fists do the talking.
744. Whenever it doesn't rain enough, the earth just has to make dew.
745. Shout out to the guy who just missed three good pitches in baseball...
746. My girlfriend bakes a mean homemade pretzel, but with a twist.
747. I have loads of fun doing laundry.
748. Vacuuming really sucks.
749. I was once addicted to line dancing so bad, I had to enter a two-step program.
750. I've told you all a million times not to exaggerate!
751. Petting zoos are a great place to pick up chicks.
752. My Chapstick is so cool, it's the balm!
753. It was supposed to rain today, but it mist.
754. I was worried about my speeding ticket, but I now know it's all fine.
755. I wasn't planning to puke, but then something came up.
756. Geology is as hard as a rock.
757. He was losing the farting contest, but he got a second wind.
758. Cannibals are just people who are fed up with people.
759. One morning I shot an elephant in my pajamas. How he got in my pajamas, I don't know.
760. I won't apologize and I'm sorry if you have a problem with that.
761. The worst part of being so tall is that my jokes go right over most peoples' head.
762. If you are feeling cold, you should sit in the corner. it's always 90 degrees.
763. Every time you ingest food coloring, you dye a little inside.
764. Born free, taxed to death.
765. Whenever I find the key to success, someone changes the lock.
766. I used to like my neighbors, until they put a password on their Wi-Fi.
767. I'd like to start with the chimney jokes – I've got a stack of them. The first one is on the house.
768. I was reading a book – 'The History of Glue' – I couldn't put it down.
769. I was stealing things in the supermarket today while balanced on the shoulders of vampires. I was charged with shoplifting on three counts.
770. I'm so lazy, I've got a smoke alarm with a snooze button.
771. You know, somebody actually complimented me on my driving today. They left a little note on the windscreen, it said 'Parking Fine.' So that was nice.

772. I wrote a book on penguins. Paper would have been better.

773. I went into this video shop, and the man asked if I'd like to rent Batman Forever. I said, "No, just for two days!"

774. Why is lemon juice made with artificial flavor, and dishwashing liquid made with real lemons?

775. Why don't you ever see the headline "Psychic Wins Lottery"?

776. A man was arrested for stealing helium balloons, police held him for a while then let him go.

777. I don't know why I don't like fragrant candles, it just doesn't make scents.

778. Someone handing out flyers on a street corner is basically like them saying, "Here, throw this away."

779. A guy walks into a bar... and it hurt.

780. I couldn't work out how to fasten my seatbelt...Then it clicked!

781. I don't trust people with graph paper...They're always plotting something!

782. I was thirsty, so I went to Kroger to buy 8 Sprites. When I got home, I realized that I had only picked 7 up!

783. A new type of broom has been released...It's sweeping the nation!

784. Honk if you like peace and quiet!

785. Evening news is where they begin with 'Good evening', and then proceed to tell you why it isn't.

786. It's not that I'm afraid to die...I just don't want to be there when it happens.

787. I want patience...And I want it, NOW!

788. If a synchronized swimmer drowns, do the rest of them have to?

789. Two guys walked into a bar - the third one ducked.

790. I love sign language. it's very handy!

791. I'm the kind of guy who stops the microwave at 1 second just to feel like a bomb diffuser.

792. I saw that show, '50 Things To Do Before You Die'. I would have thought the obvious one was "Shout For Help".

793. Bill Gates farted in an apple store and stank up the place. But it's their own fault because they don't have Windows.

794. I totally understand how batteries feel because I'm rarely ever included in things either.

795. We live in a society where pizza gets to your house faster than the police.

796. Last night I dreamed I ate a ten-pound marshmallow, and when I woke up my pillow was gone.

797. Police arrested two kids yesterday, one was drinking battery acid, the other was eating fireworks. They charged one and let the other one off.

798. If you find yourself in a hole, you should stop digging.

799. I always keep my dreams alive; that's why I hit the snooze button a lot.

800. If winning isn't everything, why do they keep score?

801. I was wondering why glass was transparent, then it became clear to me.

802. I don’t mean to brag, but I just completed my 21-day diet in 4 hours and 30 minutes.
803. Living on Earth is expensive, but it does include a free trip around the sun.
804. I love my life, but it just wants to be friends.
805. Wi-Fi went down during family dinner tonight, one kid started talking and I didn’t know who he was.
806. These mousetraps would probably work a lot better if I didn’t like cheese so much.
807. Shotgun wedding: A case of wife or death.
808. A grenade thrown into a kitchen in France would result in Linoleum Blownapart.
809. My dog used to chase people on a bike a lot. It got so bad, finally I had to take his bike away.
810. My boss told me to have a good day... So, I went home.
811. The other day, my wife asked me to pass her lipstick but I accidentally passed her a glue stick. She still isn't talking to me.
812. When you look closely, all mirrors look like eyeballs.
813. I just wrote a book on reverse psychology. Do *not* read it!
814. As I suspected, someone has been adding soil to my garden. The plot thickens.
815. When a deaf person sees someone yawn do they think it’s a scream?
816. I get enough exercise pushing my luck.
817. I don’t suffer from insanity, I enjoy every minute of it.
818. A balanced diet means a cupcake in each hand.
819. I think the worst time to have a heart attack is during a game of charades.
820. My wallet is like an onion. When I open it, it makes me cry...
821. I'm not clumsy, the floor just hates me, the table and chairs are bullies and the walls get in my way.
822. I don’t play soccer because I enjoy the sport. I’m just doing it for kicks.
823. I’ve never gone to a gun range before. I decided to give it a shot!
824. I thought about going on an all-almond diet. But that's just nuts!
825. The rotation of earth really makes my day.
826. I would avoid the sushi if I was you. It’s a little fishy.
827. This graveyard looks overcrowded. People must be dying to get in there.
828. The shovel was a ground-breaking invention.
829. Santa Claus' favorite swimming spot is the North Pool.
830. Santa was forced to attend a Christmas party because his presents was required.
831. I love when candy canes are in mint condition.
832. I have an EpiPen. My friend gave it to me when he was dying, it seemed very important to him that I have it.
833. I told my friend 10 jokes to get him to laugh. Sadly, no pun in 10 did.
834. As a scarecrow, people say I’m outstanding in my field. But hay, it’s in my jeans.
835. I never make mistakes...I thought I did once; but I was wrong.
836. Old quarterbacks never die. They just pass away.
837. My friend asked me to help him round up his 37 sheep. I said "40".
838. The universe is made of 4 things, protons, electrons, neutrons and morons.

839. Do birds really “sing” or are they releasing tiny screams because they’re scared of heights?

840. Went to a petting zoo last week with only 1 dog. It was a shitzu,

841. Just seen an idiot in my local gym putting a bottle of water into the Pringles holder on the treadmill.

842. Who cleans up after guide dogs?

843. If a parrot can recite the Lord’s Prayer does that make it a bird of prey?

844. When I was a child I wanted to be a web designer. I’ve always had a fascination with spiders.

845. Can’t believe how awesome my new pet goldfish is. Just found out that if you put it on the carpet it can do break dancing.

846. My doctor told me today I need to watch my drinking. I now drink in front of a mirror.

847. Diet Day 1: Just removed all the fattening food from my house, it was delicious.

848. A funeral was held today for the inventor of air conditioning. Thousands of fans attended.

849. When you have a fat friend at school, see-saws no longer exist, only catapults.

850. The worst part about getting fired from my job at the unemployment office was that I still had to show up the next day.

851. Someone really close to me died yesterday. Luckily the train wasn’t very busy so I just moved seats.

852. I used to have a fear of climbing walls but I’ve finally managed to get over it.

853. In the morning I like to do 7 sit ups. It’s not a lot but my alarm clock only allows you to press snooze so many times.

854. I’ve always wanted to be a doctor, but I’ve never had the patience...

855. Driving a sports car and staying under the speed limit is like going to McDonalds for a salad.

856. I used to have a job repairing lifts. It had its ups and downs.

857. Definition of Wisdom: The thing that happens when you run out of stupid ideas.

858. I wish I went to boarding school as a kid... Would love to be able to surf.

859. Just been sacked from my new job at Starbucks. Apparently ground coffee isn’t supposed to contain any dirt from the ground.

860. Have you heard about that new coffee that makes you tired and unhappy? It’s called depresso.

861. Some people are ridiculous. There are 363 days left till Christmas and people already have their Christmas lights up.

862. Went to the barbers today and had a no. 2. At first it just seemed like a fart but I ended up following through.

863. Every time I hear the dirty word 'exercise,' I wash my mouth out with chocolate.

864. A dog gave birth to puppies near the road and was cited for littering.

865. I tried to convince my little girl that it’s perfectly normal to accidentally poop your pants. ... But she didn’t buy it. She’s still making fun of me.

866. My wife says I'm addicted to auctions but she's wrong. I stopped after going once... going twice...
867. I was forced to swallow purple food coloring. I feel violated.
868. You know what they say about grandfather clocks... They're old timers.
869. I accidentally sent my friend flowers over the internet. Whoops, E-Daisies.
870. I used to be a member of the secret cooking society. They kicked me out for spilling the beans.
871. I recently got a step ladder. It hurts not being able to see my real ladder anymore.
872. I dreamed I drowned in an ocean made of orange soda. When I woke up I realized it was just a Fanta sea.
873. I like jokes. But jokes about air conditioners? Not a fan.
874. My friend has been a limo driver for 25 years and hasn't had a single customer. All that time and nothing to chauffeur it.
875. I'm addicted to seaweed. I must seek kelp.
876. I know every digit of pi. Just not in the right order.
877. I'm not saying my wife's a bad cook... But she uses the smoke alarm as a timer.
878. 3D printers are now printing guns. That's nothing though. I've had a Canon printer for years.
879. My neighbors are listening to great music. Whether they like it or not.
880. My doctor loves hitting my knee to test my reflexes... He really gets a kick out of it.
881. I've started a boat building business in my attic. The sails are going through the roof.
882. Prison may be just one word... But to some, it's a whole sentence.
883. I can always tell, just by looking, when someone is lying. I can also tell when they're standing.
884. I got a parking ticket for being parked illegally. I've no idea why. The sign clearly said, "Fine for parking".
885. Never give a donation to anyone collecting for a marathon. They'll take the money and run.
886. To this day, the boy who used to bully me at school still takes my lunch money. On the plus side, he makes great Subway sandwiches.
887. I finally managed to get rid of that nasty electric charge I've been carrying. I'm ex-static!
888. I've started a business where I weigh tiny objects. It's a small-scale operation.
889. I had a game of quiet tennis today. It's just like regular tennis but without the racket.
890. I hate people that always need assurance. Do you know what I mean?
891. I ordered a thesaurus from Amazon... But when it was delivered all the pages were blank. I have no words to describe how angry I am.
892. I'm combining Easter and April Fool's day this year. I'm sending the kids out to look for eggs I haven't hidden.

893. Humpty Dumpty always had a terrible summer. At least he had a great fall.

894. I'm in so much debt, I can't afford to pay my electric bill. These are the darkest days of my life.
895. If you struggle cutting cake... Is it still a piece of cake?
896. My friend rang me and asked me what I was doing... I said, "Probably failing my driving test."
897. I just farted in my wallet. Now I have gas money.
898. I dropped my phone from the 21st floor of a building yesterday. Good thing it was in airplane mode.
899. Bill Gates has offered to pay for Trump's wall. On the condition he gets to install windows.
900. I got fired from my job as a chef for stealing kitchen equipment. It was a whisk I was willing to take.
901. The invention of the shovel was groundbreaking... But the invention of the broom swept the nation.
902. Poop jokes may not be my favorite type of joke. But they're a solid number two.
903. I get so angry when I see someone with their wallet chained to their belt. I just can't take it.
904. I'll do algebra, I'll do statistics, even trigonometry ... But graphing is where I draw the line.
905. I turned 18 today... and to celebrate I bought a locket and put my own picture in it. I guess I really am in-de-pendant.
906. To the guy who found my empty wallet... I don't know how to repay you.
907. I introduced my new girlfriend to my family today. My kids liked her, but my wife seemed kind of mad.
908. My wife found out I was cheating after she found the letters I was hiding. She got mad and said she's never playing Scrabble with me again.
909. I saw a sign that said, "Falling rocks". I tried. It doesn't.
910. I tried to change my password to "14days". The computer said it was two week.
911. Not all math puns are bad. Just sum.
912. I've fallen in love with a pencil and we're getting married. I can't wait to introduce my parents to my bride 2B.
913. When I noticed "HI" in the alphabet ... I thought someone was going to be my friend. Then I saw the next two letters.
914. My astronaut girlfriend has dumped me... She said she needs space.
915. I just entered a stair climbing competition. I guess I'd better step up my game.
916. At my new job, I have 500 people under me. I mow the grass at the cemetery.
917. 4, 6, 8 and 9 have all been murdered. 2, 3, 5 and 7 are the prime suspects.
918. Yesterday I accidentally swallowed some food coloring. The doctor says I'm OK, but I feel like I've dyed a little inside.
919. My friends got a butler who's got no left arm. Serves him right.
920. A guy just assaulted me with milk, cream and butter. How dairy!
921. I just replaced my shoelaces with earphones. Now they tie themselves.

922. My ultra-sensitive toothpaste gets jealous when I use other toothpastes.
923. I can't stand being in a wheelchair.
924. I played triangle in a reggae band but left – it was just one ting after another.
925. It's a disgrace that gingerbread men are forced to live in houses made of their own flesh.
926. I make the little things count – I teach math to midgets.
927. If I save time, when do I get it back?
928. A pedestrian hit me and went under my car.
929. Only in America... do banks leave both doors open and then chain the pens to the counters.
930. Why are they called apartments when they are all stuck together?
931. Why is the time of day with the slowest traffic called rush hour?
932. When an employment application asks who is to be notified in case of emergency, I always write, "A very good doctor".
933. Intelligence is like underwear. It is important that you have it, but not necessary that you show it off.
934. Why don't sheep shrink when it rains?
935. If someone with multiple personalities threatens to kill himself, is it considered a hostage situation?
936. My aunt died, God bless her, at a ripe old age of 104. We called her Aunt Tique.
937. If milk goes bad if not refrigerated, why does it not go bad inside the cow?
938. Why does caregiver and caretaker mean the same thing?
939. Do Siamese twins pay for one ticket or two tickets when they go to movies and concerts?
940. How can something be "new" and "improved"? if it's new, what was it improving on?
941. If a doctor suddenly had a heart attack while doing surgery, would the other doctors work on the doctor or the patient?
942. Why does quicksand work slowly?
943. Can you daydream at night?
944. If God sneezes, what should you say?
945. How do you handcuff a one-armed man?
946. What was Captain Hook's name before he got the hook?
947. Why do people say they "slept like a baby" when babies wake up every few hours?
948. Do dentists go to other dentists or do they just do it themselves?
949. If parents say, "Never take candy from strangers" then why do we celebrate Halloween?
950. Can a cemetery raise its prices and blame it on the cost of living?
951. Do coffins have lifetime guarantees?
952. Why do they call them "Free Gifts"? Aren't all gifts free?
953. Are children who act in rated 'R' movies allowed to see them?
954. Why do people say, "heads up" when you should duck?
955. If a deaf person must go to court, is it still called a hearing?

956. Why is it that no matter what color bubble bath you use the bubbles are always white?
957. Do pigs pull their ham strings?
958. When sign makers go on strike, is anything written on their signs?
959. If one synchronized swimmer drowns, should the rest of them drown too?
960. Do the Alphabet song and Twinkle, Twinkle Little Star have the same tune?
961. If a vacuum cleaner really sucks, is that good or bad?
962. If people with one arm go to get their nails done, do they pay half price?
963. How do you tell when you run out of invisible ink?
964. Could someone ever get addicted to counseling? If so, how would you treat them?
965. Can bald men get lice?
966. Why do 'fat chance' and 'slim chance' mean the same thing?
967. How does the guy who drives the snowplow get to work in the morning?
968. When French people swear, do they say, "pardon my English?"
969. Why do they call it quicksand when it sucks you down slowly?
970. Why do we call something sent by car a shipment and something sent by ship a cargo?
971. Why do we sing "Take me out to the ball game," when we are already there?
972. If space is a vacuum, who changes the bags?
973. If you can't drink and drive, why do bars have parking lots?
974. Why doesn't glue stick to the inside of the bottle?
975. Why is the third hand on the watch called a second hand?
976. If a cow laughed, would milk come out her nose?
977. Why do they call it a TV "set" when you only get one?
978. If a book about failures doesn't sell, is it a success?
979. If knees were backwards, what would chairs look like?
980. What is a "free" gift? Aren't all gifts free?
981. Why is the alphabet in that order? Is it because of that song?
982. How can you chop down a tree and then chop it up?
983. Why do you press harder on the buttons of a remote control when you know the batteries are dead?
984. Can you sentence a homeless man to house arrest?
985. Why is the blackboard green?
986. What happens if someone loses a lost and found box?
987. How do you throw away a garbage can?
988. If croutons are stale bread, why do they come in airtight packages?
989. Do fish get thirsty?
990. Can you cry under water?
991. Why do they call it 'chili' if it's hot?
992. Why do we call them restrooms when no one goes there to rest?
993. Why do sleeping pills have warning labels that state: Caution - May Cause Drowsiness?
994. Why are they called "stands" when they're made for sitting?

995. If you only have one eye...are you blinking or winking?
996. What is shaved ice? Did it have hair on it before it was shaved?
997. Why do hot dogs come in packages of ten while hot dog buns come in packages of just eight?
998. Why is it called a "hamburger" if there's no ham?
999. Why are there interstate highways in Hawaii?

Pick Up Lines

1000. Roses are red and violets are blue there's nothing in the world prettier than you
1001. I'm not a hoarder but I really want to keep you forever.
1002. You remind me of an overdue library book, because you got Fine written all over you.
1003. Roses are red, I have a crush, whenever I'm around you, all I do is blush.
1004. Roses are red, violets are blue, lava is hot and so are you.
1005. I heard you're good in algebra, can you replace my X without asking Y?
1006. You are hotter than the bottom of my laptop.
1007. I'm no organ donor, but I'd be happy to give you my heart.
1008. If I were a cat, I'd spend all 9 lives with you.
1009. Can I punch you in the face... with my lips?
1010. Your lips look so lonely...Would they like to meet mine?
1011. You must be Jamaican, because Jamaican me crazy.
1012. You must be a hell of a thief because you stole my heart from across the room.
1013. You might be asked to leave soon. You are making the other women look bad.
1014. Was your father a mechanic? Then how did you get such a finely tuned body?
1015. Was that an earthquake or did you just rock my world?
1016. You're so sweet, you're giving me a toothache.
1017. Hey, my name's Microsoft. Can I crash at your place tonight?
1018. Good thing I just bought term life insurance ... because I saw you and my heart stopped!
1019. Do you believe in love at first sight or should I walk past again?
1020. If you were a vegetable, you'd be a cutecumber.
1021. Did you hear of the new disease called beautiful, I think you're infected?
1022. If you were words on a page, you'd be fine print.
1023. Kiss me if I'm wrong, but dinosaurs still exist, right?
1024. If you were a triangle you'd be acute one.
1025. I know this is going to sound cheesy, but I think you're the gratest.
1026. Do your legs hurt from running through my dreams all night?
1027. Hey, tie your shoes! I don't want you falling for anyone else.
1028. You must be Jamaican, because Jamaican me crazy.
1029. There is something wrong with my cell phone. It doesn't have your number in it.
1030. If nothing lasts forever, will you be my nothing?
1031. I must be in a museum, because you truly are a work of art.
1032. You spend so much time in my mind, I should charge you rent.
1033. We're not socks. But I think we'd make a great pair.

1034. Kiss me if I'm wrong, but dinosaurs still exist, right?

1035. Our time together is like a nap, it just doesn't last long enough.

1036. If you were a basketball, I'd never pass because I want to keep you all to myself.

1037. There's only one thing I would change about you, your last name.

www.ingramcontent.com/pod-product-compliance
Ingram Content Group UK Ltd.
Pitfield, Milton Keynes, MK11 3LW, UK
UKHW041901190726
13854UKWH00003B/1010

9 781387 277483